# SPACE TELESCOPES

## INSTAGRAM OF THE STARS

### ANDREW LANGLEY

CONTENT CONSULTANT
SARAH RUIZ
Aerospace Engineer

CAPSTONE PRESS
a capstone imprint

Edge Books are published by Capstone Press,
1710 Roe Crest Drive, North Mankato, Minnesota 56003
www.capstonepub.com

Library of Congress Cataloging-in-Publication Data
Names: Langley, Andrew, 1949– author.
Title: Space telescopes : instagram of the stars / by Andy Langley. Description: North Mankato,
Minnesota : Capstone Press, [2019] | Series: Edge books. Future space | "Edge Books is published
by Capstone Press." | Audience: Ages 8–9. | Audience: K to grade 3. Identifiers: LCCN 2019004842|
ISBN 9781543572711 (hardcover) | ISBN 9781543575194 (pbk.) | ISBN 9781543572797 (ebook pdf)
Subjects: LCSH: Hubble Space Telescope (Spacecraft)—Juvenile literature. | Space telescopes—
Juvenile literature. | Outer space—Exploration—Juvenile literature. Classification: LCC
QB500.268 .L365 2019 | DDC 522/.2919—dc23
LC record available at https://lccn.loc.gov/2019004842

Editorial Credits
Michelle Parkin, editor; Laura Mitchell, designer; Jo Miller, media researcher;
Katy LaVigne, production specialist

Photo Credits
NASA, 8, 9 (Top), 11, 12, 24, Desiree Stover, 23, JPL-Caltech, Cover (telescope), 9 (Bottom), 16;
Newscom: NOTIMEX/CORTESÍA, 6, Polaris, 28, Reuters/Mike Hutchings, 19, SIPA/Chine Nouvelle, 21;
Science Source: Carlos Clarivan, 15, European Southern Observatory/L. Calcada, 27; Shutterstock:
robert_s, Cover (Earth), siraphat, 5; Wikimedia: Benjamín Núñez González, 18

Design Elements
Capstone; Shutterstock: Audrius Birbilas

Printed and bound in the United States of America.
PA70

# TABLE OF CONTENTS

# CHAPTER ONE

# EYES ON THE UNIVERSE

On a clear night, point your phone up at the sky and take a picture. Click! How does it look? Pretty murky and spotty. Try it again. This time zoom in as far as you can. Click! Is that any better? Not really. The planets and stars are too far away.

Imagine you have a giant camera with a mega lens. Click! The photo is much clearer. Now put that giant camera on a rocket and whiz it up into space. Click! Finally, you've got an amazing photo. Like a giant camera, space telescopes can take incredible pictures of stars and other objects in space. Some giant telescopes are on the ground. Other smaller ones fly around in space.

## SPACE FACT:

Powerful rockets launch telescopes into space. When the telescope reaches Earth's orbit, the rocket detaches and falls back to the ground.

Proxima Centauri is the nearest star to our sun.

PROXIMA CENTAURI ◎

## SPACE FACT:

Your TV's remote control uses infrared rays to change the channel.

# SIGNALS FROM SPACE

The closest star to our sun is called Proxima Centauri. It's 4.2 **light-years** away. That's more than 24 trillion miles (38.6 trillion kilometers)! It's impossible for us to see with the naked eye. But it's no problem using space telescopes. They can snap images of that star and others like it that are even farther away. Using communication systems, telescopes then transmit the data back to Earth.

But how do telescopes capture these images? A star gives out rays of energy called **radiation**. Telescopes capture the star's image by picking up this radiation. Then the data is sent to scientists on Earth. But it's not as simple as it sounds. There are many kinds of radiation. We can see some radiation, such as light rays. Other radiation, such as **infrared** rays, we can't see. **X-rays** and **gamma rays** are packed with powerful energy. Each of these rays requires a different kind of telescope to detect them in space.

**gamma ray**—a powerful form of radiation that comes from stars and other space bodies

**infrared**—a type of energy, such as heat, that cannot be seen by the human eye

**light-year**—a unit for measuring distance in space; a light-year is the distance that light travels in one year

**radiation**—emission of energy in the form of waves or particles through space

**X-ray**—invisible energy waves from stars and other space bodies

# SPACE TELESCOPES OF THE PAST

Scientists have been launching telescopes into space for more than 50 years. Past telescopes have traveled around Earth and far out into the distant universe. Many have been launched by the National Aeronautics and Space Administration, or NASA.

The Compton Gamma Ray Observatory's mission lasted from 1991 to 2000. While in space, it sent back images that helped scientists understand gamma rays. Using the Compton, scientists also discovered a new kind of galaxy powered by monster **black holes**.

Compton Gamma Ray Observatory

## SPACE FACT:

Chandra X-ray Observatory is named after Subrahmanyan Chandrasekhar, an astrophysicist who won the Nobel Prize for Physics in 1983.

**SPACE FACT:**

Even a star runs out of fuel. When this happens, the center of the star collapses in a gigantic explosion. Then the star is called a supernova.

The Chandra X-ray Observatory was launched in 1999. It's still in space. The telescope has taken pictures of **supernovas**. It also detected a halo of hot gas spinning around our galaxy.

The Spitzer Space Telescope was launched in 2003. So far the telescope's camera has snapped some of the youngest stars ever seen. It has also detected a giant, twisting dust cloud called a double helix nebula in our **galaxy**.

Spitzer Space Telescope

**black hole**—an area of space with such a strong gravitational field that not even light can escape it

**galaxy**—a cluster of millions or billions of stars, together with gas and dust, bound together by gravity

**supernova**—the explosion of a very large star at the end of its life; supernovas give off a lot of energy

# CHAPTER TWO

# THE GRANDDADDY OF THEM ALL

The Hubble Space Telescope is the most famous space telescope in the world. In April 1990, NASA launched the Hubble into space aboard the **Space Shuttle** Discovery. It's still up there today. The Hubble **orbits** around Earth, taking pictures of stars and other objects that pass by. The Hubble's mission will continue through 2025.

## SPACE FACT:

The Hubble is the only telescope that can be repaired in space. Astronauts have made five trips from Earth to fix problems and attach new parts.

The Hubble has sent back a mind-boggling mountain of images and information. Scientists receive 140 gigabits of data each week! This information has changed the way scientists look at the universe. The Hubble images have illustrated how galaxies of stars grow and change over billions of years. The Hubble has taken pictures of dying stars. Scientists also discovered four icy moons that orbit the **dwarf planet** Pluto.

**dwarf planet**—space sphere that orbits the sun but has not cleared the orbit of neighboring planets

**orbit**—to travel around an object in space

**space shuttle**—a spacecraft that is meant to carry astronauts and equipment into space and back to Earth

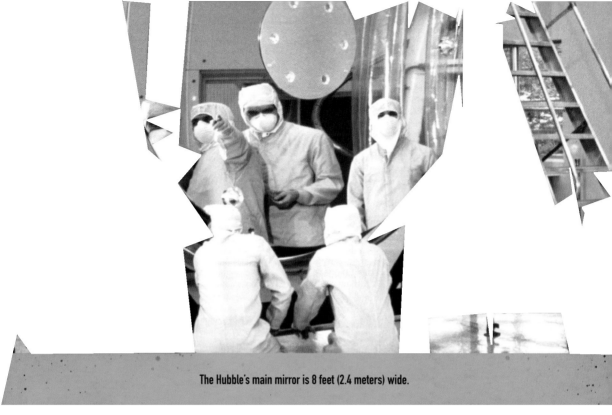

The Hubble's main mirror is 8 feet (2.4 meters) wide.

How does the Hubble Space Telescope capture amazing photos? By collecting light. Space telescopes have mirrors. In the Hubble, a star's light strikes the telescope's large main mirror. The light bounces off and hits a second, smaller mirror. The smaller mirror gathers the light into a tiny beam. The beam travels inside the telescope. There, scientific equipment analyzes the light and collects data. To retrieve this data, scientists use NASA's Space Network. This network uses satellites that work as a relay system to send and receive information from the Hubble in space.

The Hubble Space Telescope is powered by the sun. Huge panels on the sides collect **solar energy**. But what happens when the sun's light is blocked out? The telescope uses the solar energy stored in batteries. This way it never runs out of power.

**solar energy**—heat and light made by the sun

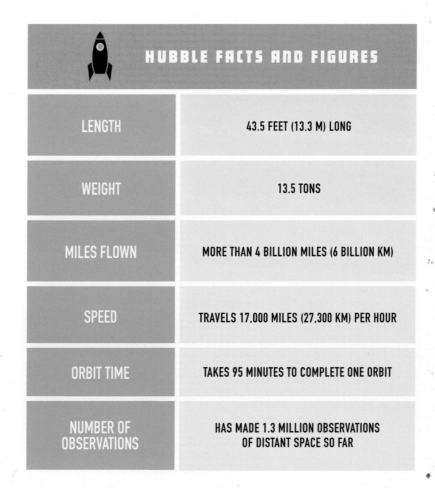

| HUBBLE FACTS AND FIGURES | |
| --- | --- |
| LENGTH | 43.5 FEET (13.3 M) LONG |
| WEIGHT | 13.5 TONS |
| MILES FLOWN | MORE THAN 4 BILLION MILES (6 BILLION KM) |
| SPEED | TRAVELS 17,000 MILES (27,300 KM) PER HOUR |
| ORBIT TIME | TAKES 95 MINUTES TO COMPLETE ONE ORBIT |
| NUMBER OF OBSERVATIONS | HAS MADE 1.3 MILLION OBSERVATIONS OF DISTANT SPACE SO FAR |

# CHAPTER THREE

# TELESCOPES NEAR AND FAR

Scientists aren't just focused on the Hubble Space Telescope. There are many other telescopes zipping through space.

NASA's Fermi Gamma-ray Space Telescope was launched in 2008. Scientists wanted to know why supermassive black holes make gamma rays. They also hoped to discover the effects gamma rays have on nearby space objects. To do this, the Fermi telescope has two special features. One is a telescope that can pinpoint thousands of sources for gamma rays. The other is a machine that records gamma ray bursts.

From 2009 to 2013, the Herschel Space Observatory was used to study the colder parts of the universe. It carried the biggest infrared telescope ever launched into space. The telescope recorded new stars being formed and clustering into new galaxies.

## SPACE FACT:

A black hole is a place where the pull of gravity is so strong that nothing can get out—even light. Supermassive black holes have been swallowing gas and other matter for billions of years.

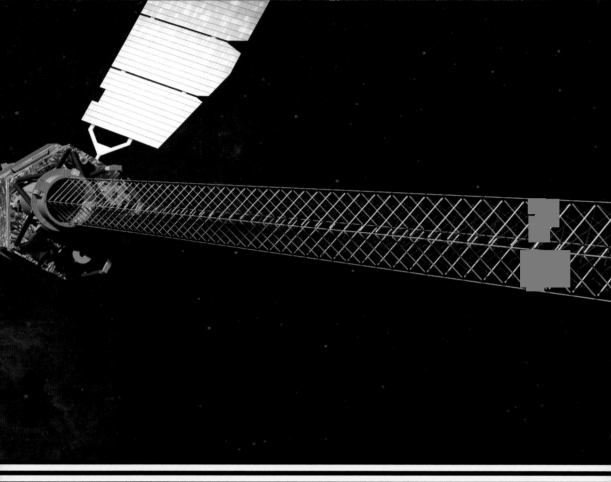

The Nuclear Spectroscopic Telescope Array, or NuSTAR, is not your typical space telescope. For starters, it was launched from an airplane. In 2012 a high-flying Lockheed Tristar airplane dropped a rocket carrying the NuSTAR. The rocket fired in mid-air and took the telescope up into space.

Using X-ray cameras, NuSTAR captured pictures of glowing fragments from exploded stars. The images were clearer than ever before.

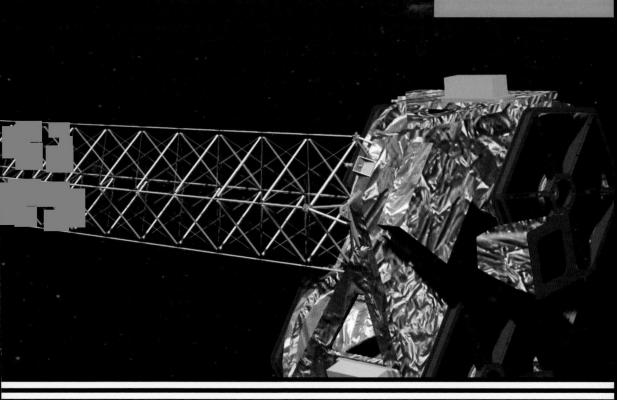

The Venus Spectral Rocket Experiment (VeSpR) had one of the shortest missions. Launched in 2013, VeSpR completed its mission in just 10 minutes. The telescope inside had one job—to study Venus's **atmosphere**. Scientists hope to learn if Venus was once covered with water.

**atmosphere**—the layer of gases that surrounds some planets, dwarf planets, and moons; Earth has an atmosphere

The GTC is one of the largest telescopes in the world. It is at the Roque de los Muchachos Observatory in Spain.

In addition to the telescopes orbiting in space, there are large telescopes here on Earth pointed at the sky. When it comes to ground telescopes, the bigger the better. These telescopes are built in places that give the clearest view of space. They have to be far away from city lights. They are often built in dry areas, such as Chile's Atacama Desert.

One of today's super giants is the Gran Telescopio Canarias (GTC) in the Canary Islands, Spain. Its main mirror is 34.1 feet (10.4 m) wide. The giant telescope gathers light from deep space. Thanks to the GTC, scientists have found a ring of stars around a distant galaxy 500 million light-years away.

The Southern African Large Telescope, or SALT, is an even bigger telescope. Located in South Africa, the telescope has a 36.4-foot (11-m) wide mirror. SALT has been used to discover five new stars in our galaxy.

SALT's mirror is made up of 91 mirror segments. Visitors saw them up close in 2005.

# TELESCOPES ON THE MOON

Telescopes on Earth take amazing images. But they have limitations. Because of Earth's rotation around the sun, ground telescopes can only watch a star for a few hours. Also, Earth's atmosphere can affect images. So what do scientists do? One option is to build telescopes on the moon. The moon has no atmosphere, so telescopes would have a clear view of space. Also, the moon spins slower than Earth. A telescope on the moon could watch the same star for 12 days.

In 2013 China's Chang'e 3 spacecraft landed on the moon. It carried a small telescope. The telescope has taken images of Earth, other galaxies, and the stars. Larger telescopes may join it soon.

### Moon Mirrors

How do you carry large and delicate telescope mirrors to the moon without breaking them? One way is to make the mirrors in space. The moon is covered in moon dust, which is made up of tiny bits of glass and other materials. Astronauts could mix this with resin to produce a very shiny material, similar to a mirror.

The Chang'e 3 captured a photo of the spacecraft's lander on the moon in 2013.

# CHAPTER FOUR

# INTO THE FUTURE

The next generation of telescopes is on the way. NASA plans to launch the James Webb Space Telescope in 2021. The James Webb will be the largest space telescope ever built. It will be as tall as a three-story house and 100 times more powerful than the Hubble!

Instead of orbiting Earth like the Hubble, the James Webb will orbit the sun—one million miles (1.6 million km) away. From this distance, scientists will be able to see where stars and galaxies were created. The telescope will also be able to capture images inside distant dust clouds, where new stars and solar systems are growing right now.

Once in space, the James Webb will unfold its mirror to catch light from the stars. The mirror is 21.3 feet (6.5 m) wide and made up of 18 segments.

### Keeping Cool

The instruments aboard the James Webb Telescope will only work if they are extremely cold. That's a big challenge when one side of the telescope is always facing the sun. To keep out the sun's heat, the James Webb carries a sunshield as big as a tennis court. In addition to keeping the telescope cool, the shield helps the telescope pick up faint light from distant stars.

LISA's three spacecraft will form a triangle in orbit.

Today's space telescopes can detect all kinds of radiation. But there is another type of energy in deep space—gravitational waves. These waves are invisible, fast ripples in space. As gravitational waves pass by, they squeeze and stretch anything in their path.

Gravitational waves are huge. Scientists need a big piece of equipment to spot them. They are building a giant space system called the Laser Interferometer Space Antenna, or LISA. It will be launched in the mid-2030s.

LISA will be made up of three spacecraft. Once in space, the three spacecraft will span an area even bigger than Earth! They will be stationed millions of miles apart and will follow Earth as it orbits the sun. The spacecraft will form a giant triangle and send signals between each other. By combining these signals, scientists will be able to detect any gravitational waves nearby.

# CHAPTER FIVE

# THE BIGGEST SCOPES EVER!

Tomorrow's telescopes won't all be in space. Advanced new ground telescopes are also planned. First up is the Large Synoptic Survey Telescope, or LSST. This is being built in the mountains of Chile. Its three giant mirrors will have a large enough field of view to photograph the entire sky every three days.

Next is something even larger—the Extremely Large Telescope (ELT). When it is complete in 2024, it will be the biggest infrared telescope in the world. The main mirror will be a whopping 127 feet (39 m) across. One of its main jobs will be to find Earth-like planets in other solar systems.

The ELT is being built on top of Cerro Armazones, a mountain in Chile.

## SPACE FACT:

The ELT's huge mirror will be made up of 798 pieces of glass. The mirror will be just 2 inches (5 centimeters) thick.

The Giant Magellan Telescope (GMT) will be up and running in Chile by 2024. The GMT will be able to collect more light than any other telescope ever built. It will be 10 times more powerful than the Hubble Space Telescope.

**SPACE FACT:**

The Atacama Desert in Chile is one of the highest and driest places on Earth. There are no clouds or pollution, giving the clearest possible view through the atmosphere.

Light from objects on the edge of space will be reflected from the GMT's mirrors into giant cameras. The cameras will identify the objects. This will help answer big questions, such as how galaxies were formed.

The biggest project of all is the Square Kilometer Array (SKA). The SKA is a radio telescope with 2,000 dishes and one million antennae. These will be spread over a huge area in South Africa and Australia. The SKA will detect radio signals from deep space, gathering much more detailed information than previous telescopes.

# GLOSSARY

atmosphere (AT-muhss-feer)—the layer of gases that surrounds some planets, dwarf planets, and moons; Earth has an atmosphere

black hole (BLAK HOHL)—an area of space with such a strong gravitational field that not even light can escape it

dwarf planet (DWAHRF PLA-nuht)—space sphere that orbits the sun but has not cleared the orbit of neighboring planets

galaxy (GAL-uhk-see)—cluster of millions or billions of stars, together with gas and dust, bound together by gravity

gamma ray (GAM-muh RAY)—a powerful form of radiation that comes from stars and other space bodies

infrared (in-fruh-RED)—a type of energy, such as heat, that cannot be seen by the human eye

light-year (LITE-yihr)—a unit for measuring distance in space; a light-year is the distance that light travels in one year

orbit (OR-bit)—to travel around an object in space

radiation (ray-dee-AY-shuhn)—emission of energy in the form of waves or particles through space

solar energy (SOH-lur Eh-nuhr-jee)—heat and light made by the sun

space shuttle (SPAYSS SHUHT-uhl)—a spacecraft that is meant to carry astronauts and equipment into space and back to Earth

supernova (soo-per-NOH-va)—the explosion of a very large star at the end of its life; supernovas give off a lot of energy

X-ray (EKS-ray)—invisible energy waves from stars and other space bodies